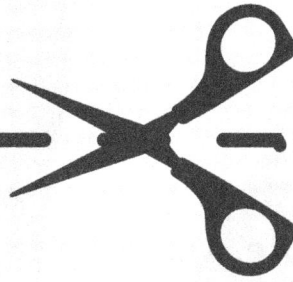

SCISSOR SKILLS

Preschool Workbook for Kids

Holding the scissors

1

Playing "it's ok".
Show the child the gesture and explain what it means. Have fun. For example, list different foods and make an upward or downward gesture. The game will prepare the child to hold the thumb up while cutting.

2

Playing with clasps.
Have fun pinning the buckles. The child will practice the movement between the thumb and other fingers.

3

Practicing the correct grip of scissors.

4

An exercise in opening and closing scissors "dry".

5

Practicing cutting in the air.

Instruction

This diary will teach you to learn how to cut with scissors, the difficulty level will increase from page to page, but don't be afraid your skills will also develop and you will be able to do it without any problems.

Have fun and be creative, learn diligently, and after completing this book you will learn to cut.

We start learning

On this page you can test your coloring supplies.

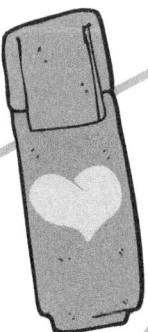

First of all, something simple: cut the paper along the line.

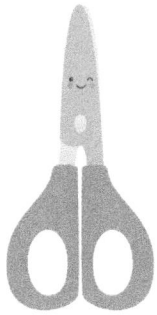

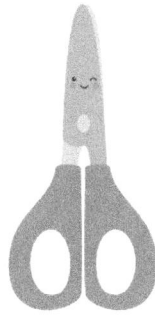

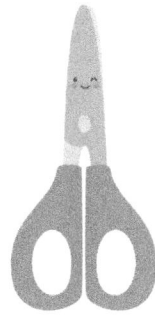

Now for something more difficult we're going to cut shapes.

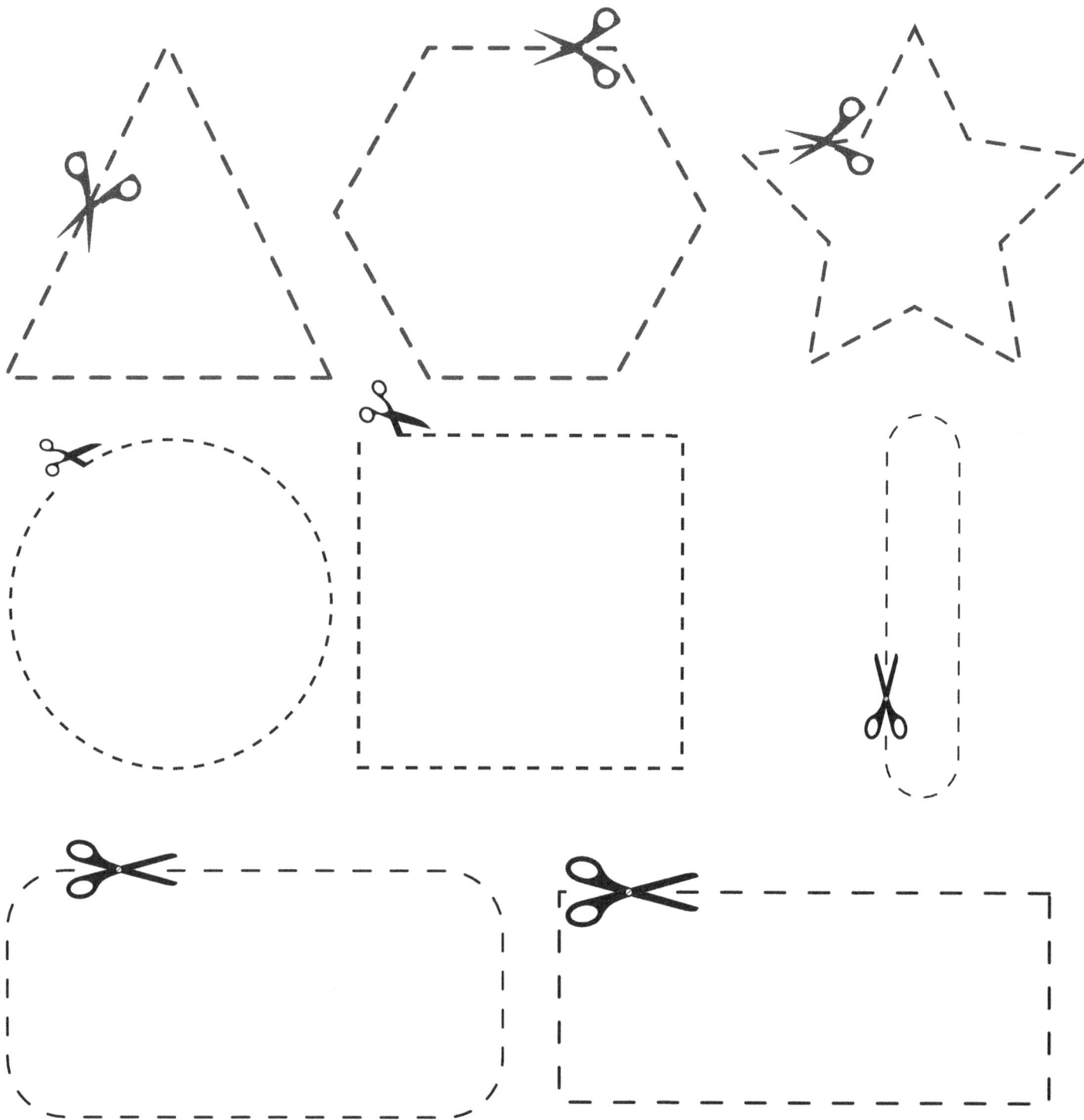

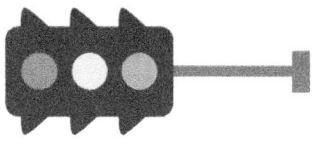

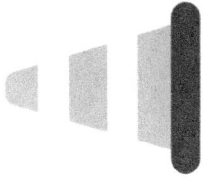

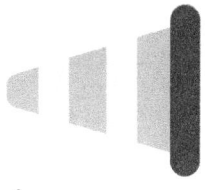

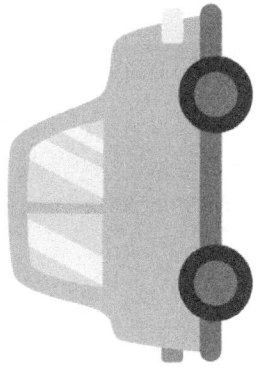

You already know the basics of cutting, now let's try something more difficult.

As this book progresses, the difficulty level will increase. Your task is to cut and paste the elements.

In this lesson, we will not only cut out but also learn to glue together what we have cut.

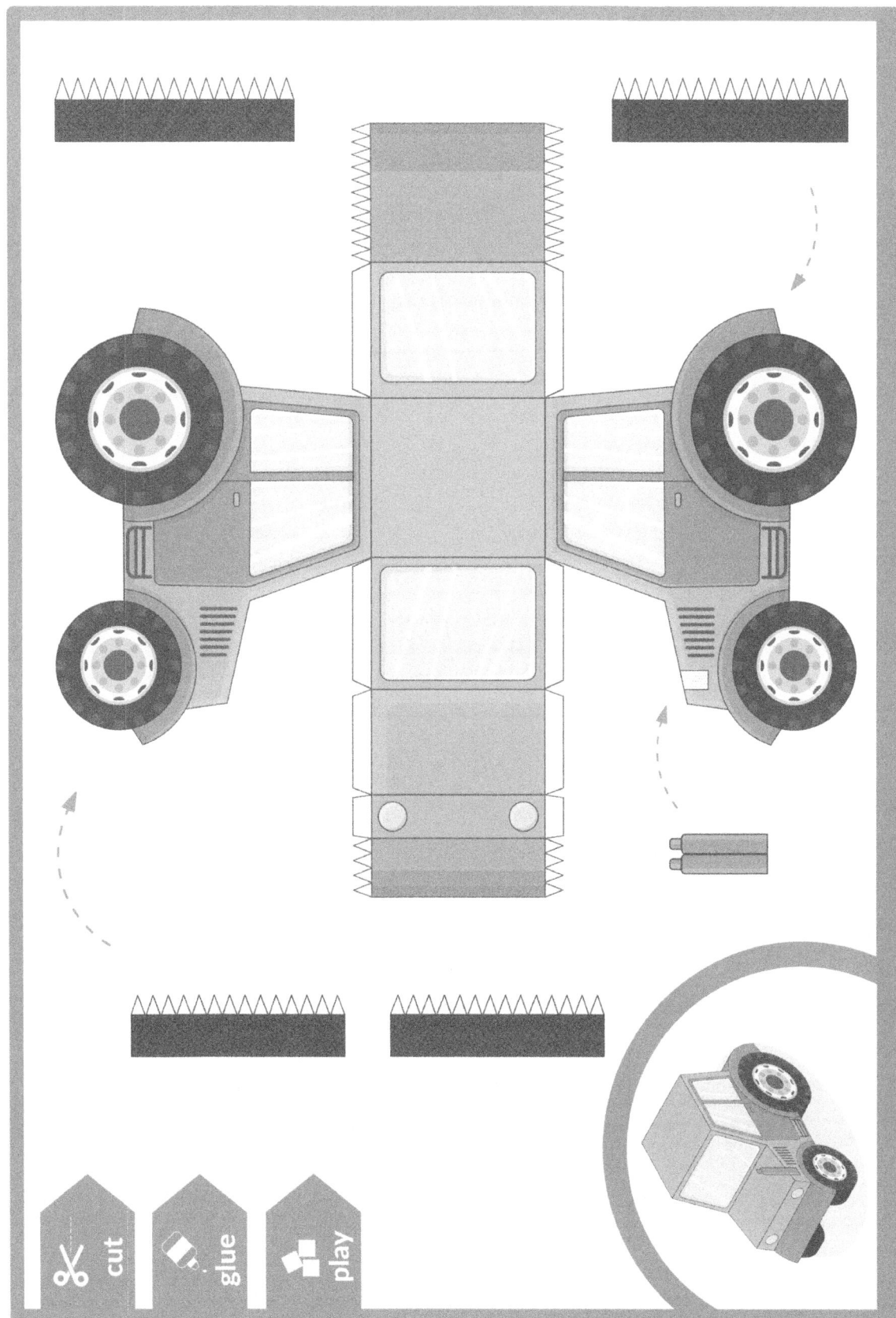

cut glue play

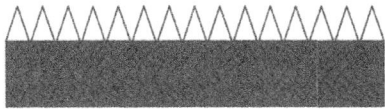
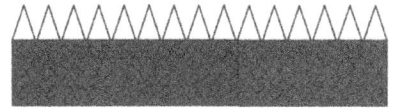
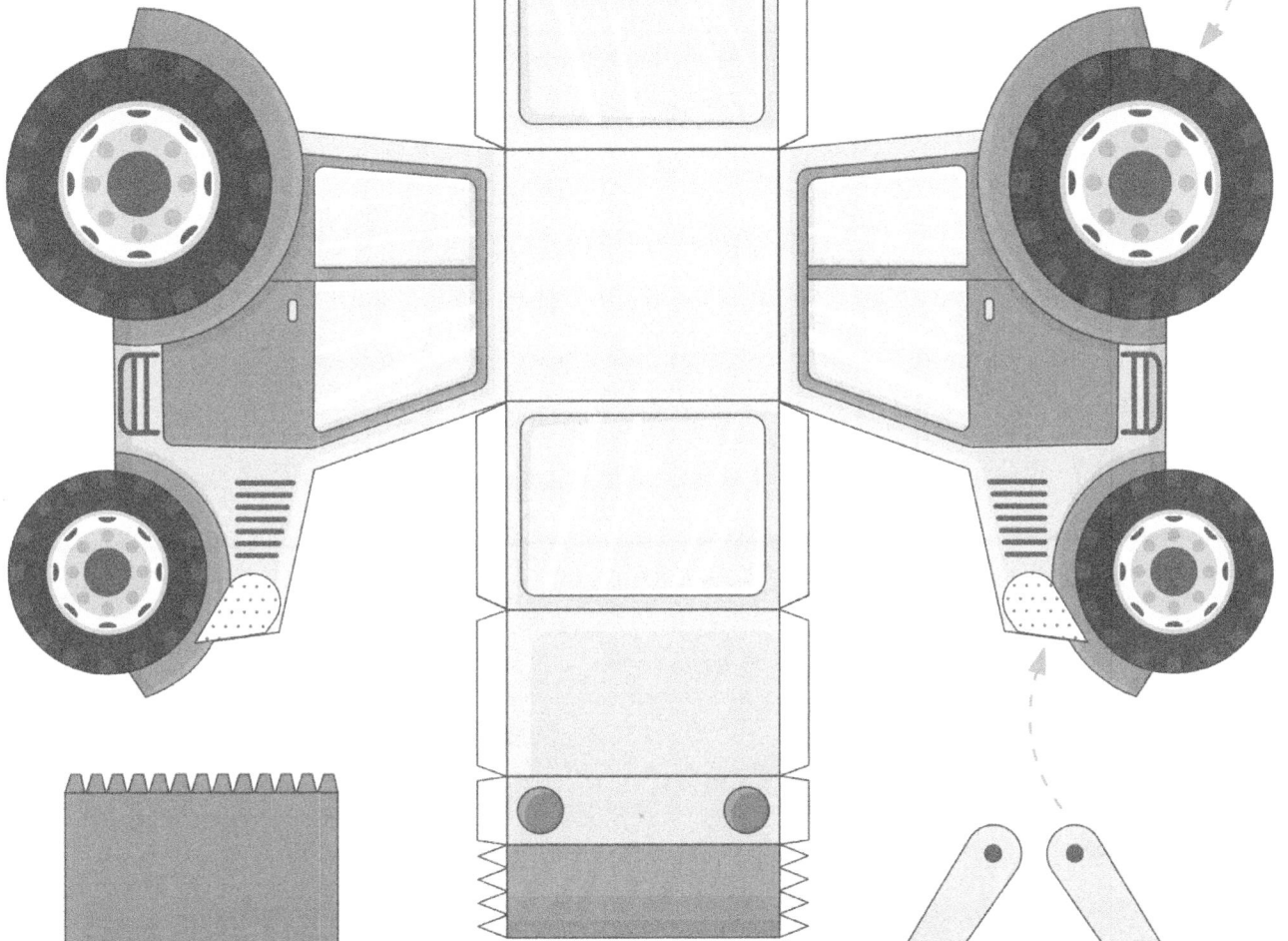
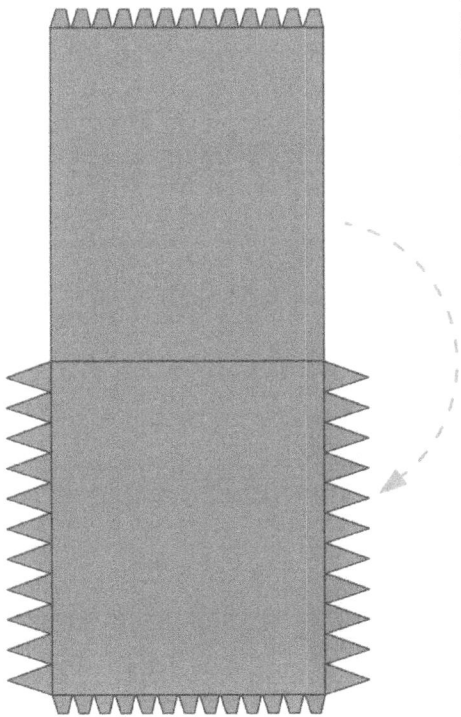
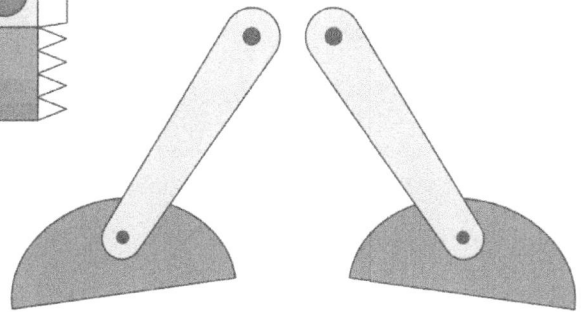
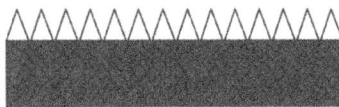
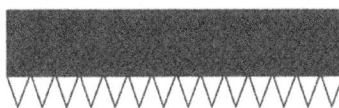

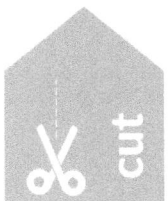 cut
 glue
 play

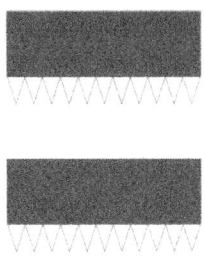
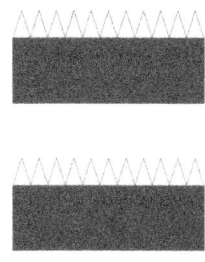
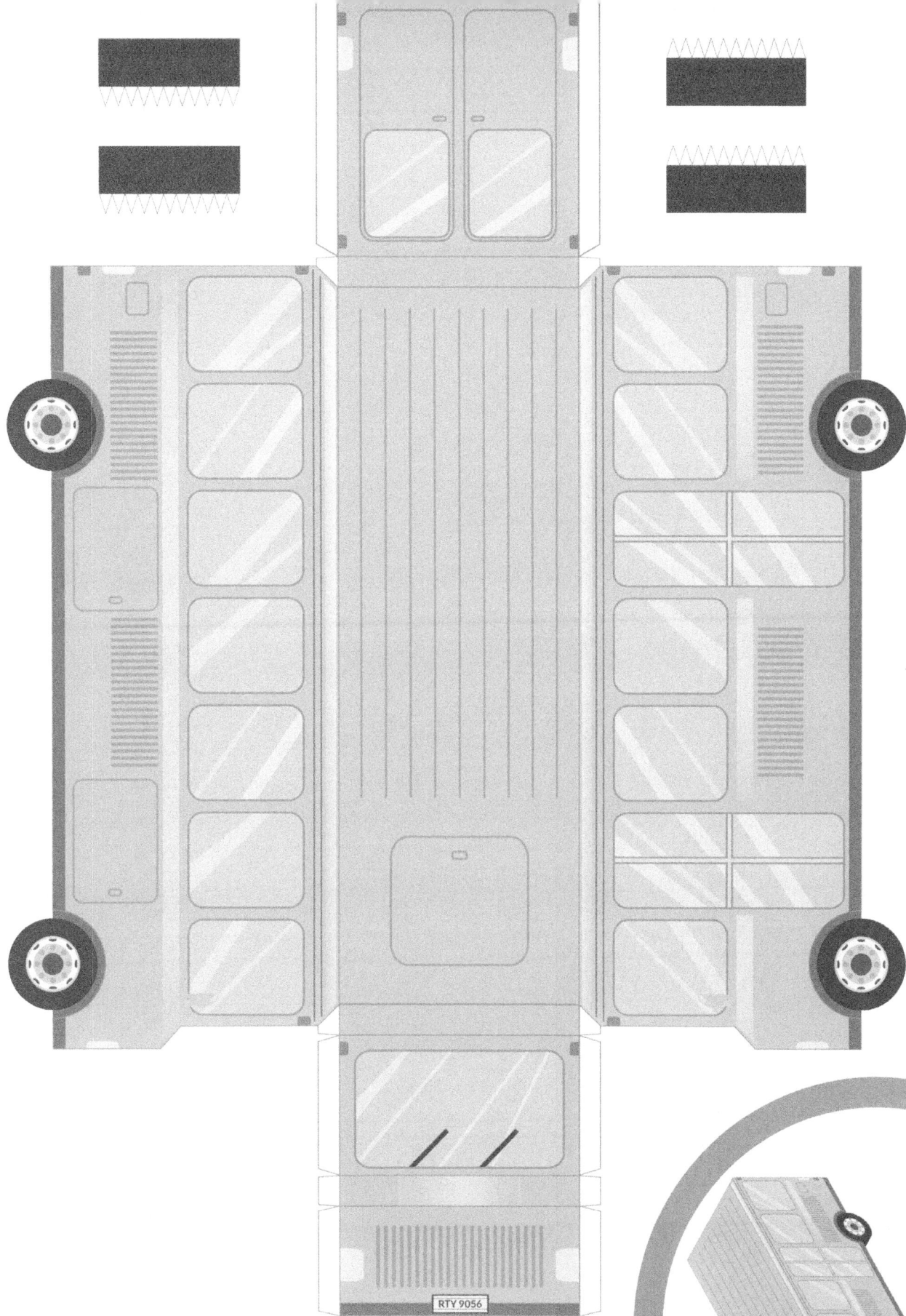

RTY 9056

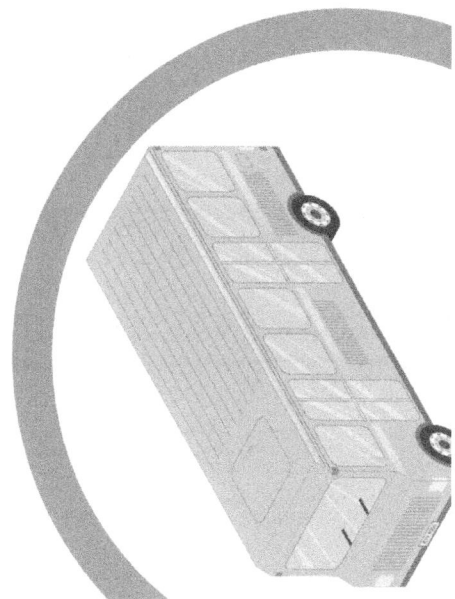

 cut

 glue

 play

Now we will make a box for your things.

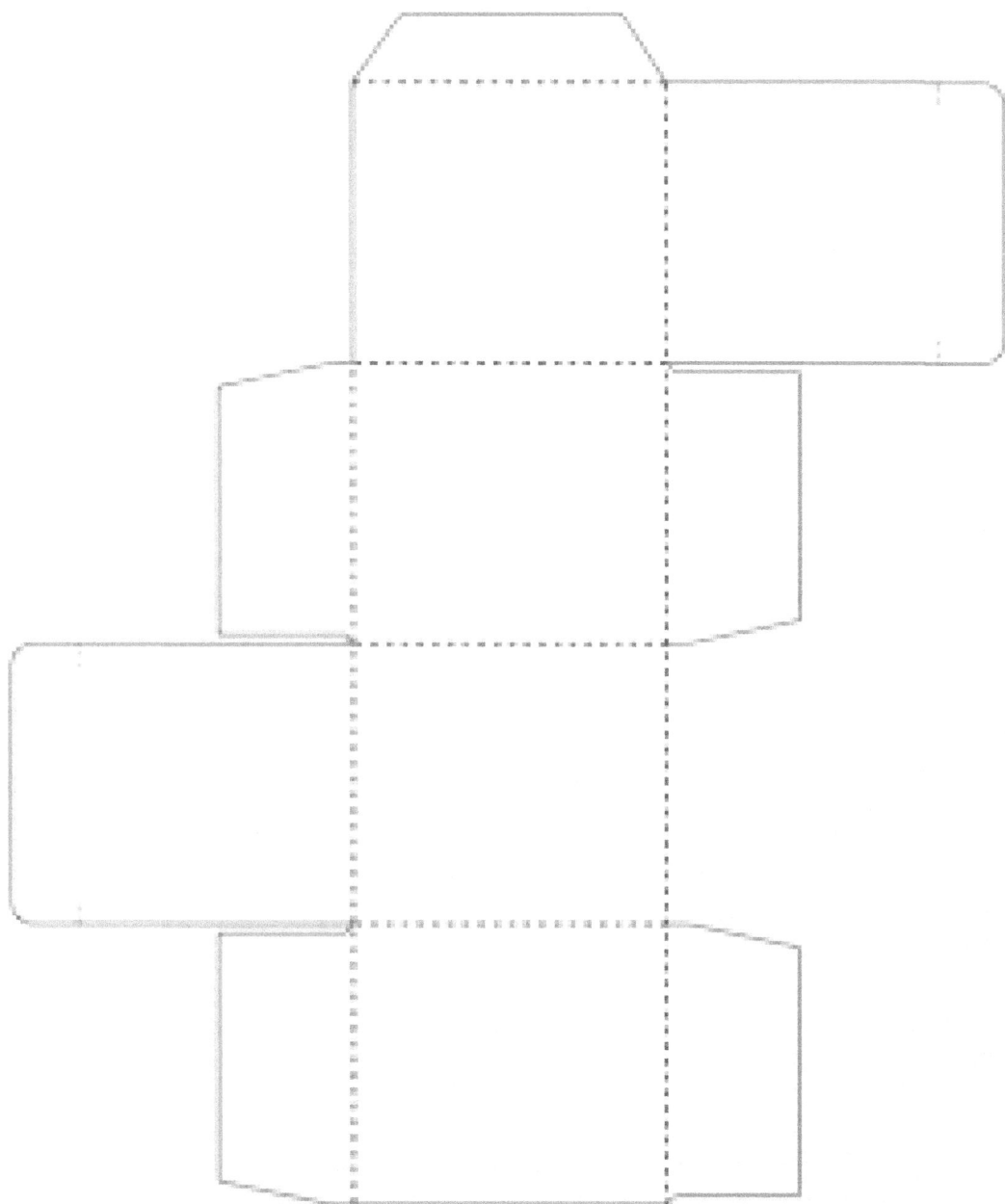

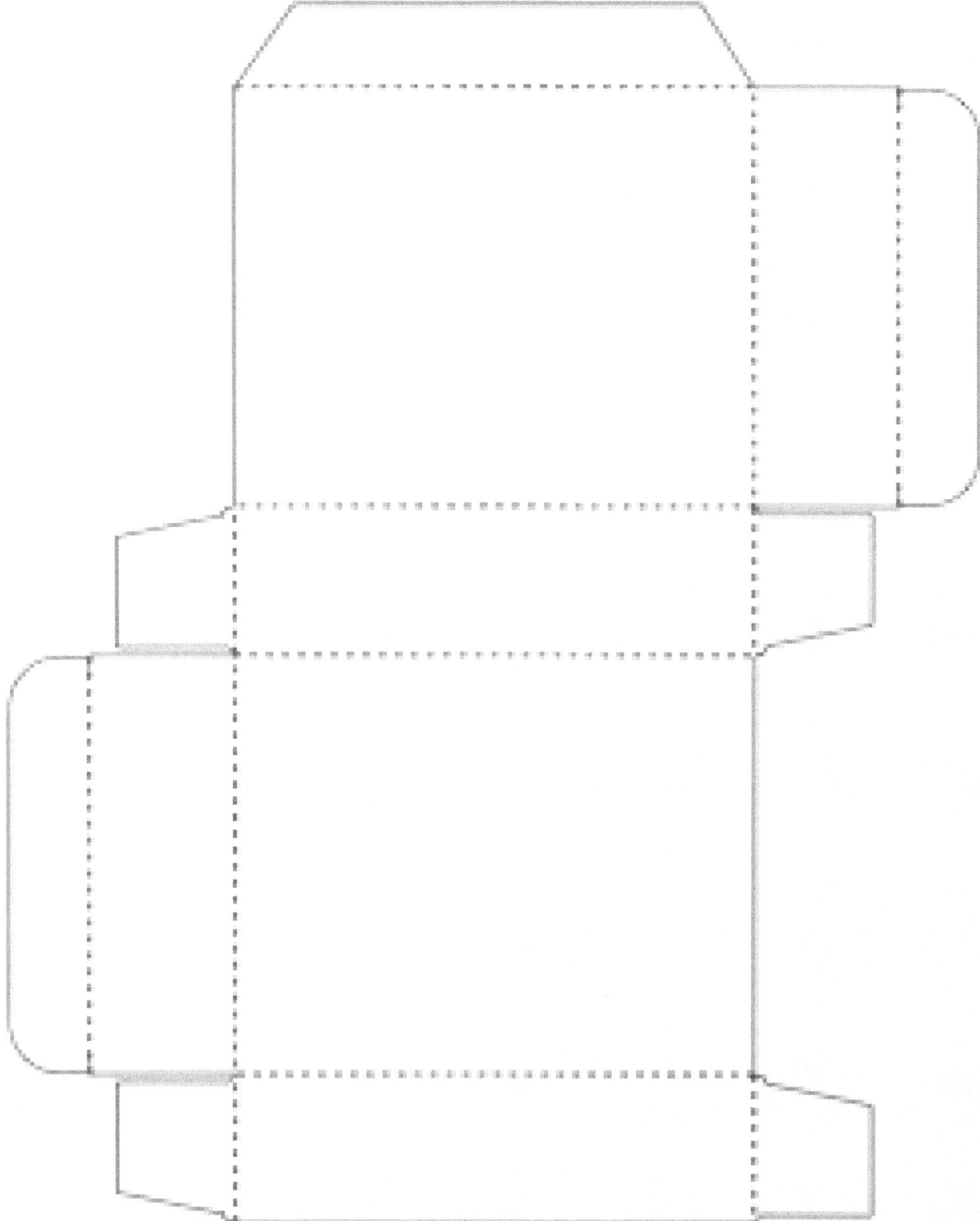

We will learn to match the numbers.

1		3		
	7	8		10
11	12			
	17	18		20

19	14	5	6	16
15	4	13	9	2

1		3		5
	7		9	
11		13		15
	17		19	

18	16	6	4	12
8	20	2	14	10

	2		4	
6		8		10
	12		14	
16		18		20

15	19	5	7	13
1	17	11	9	3

It's time for more advanced scissors.

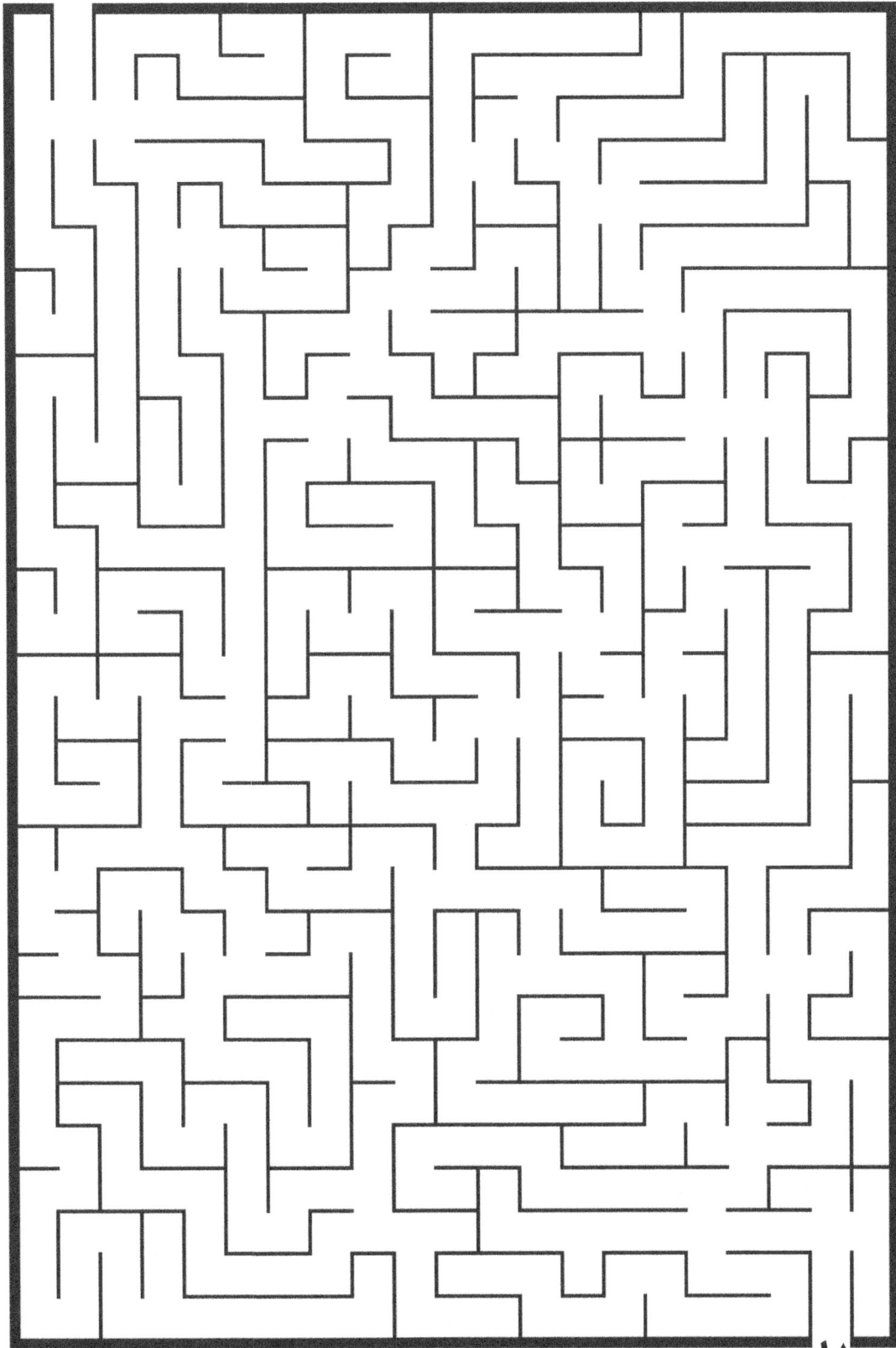

Go through the maze and then cut it out.

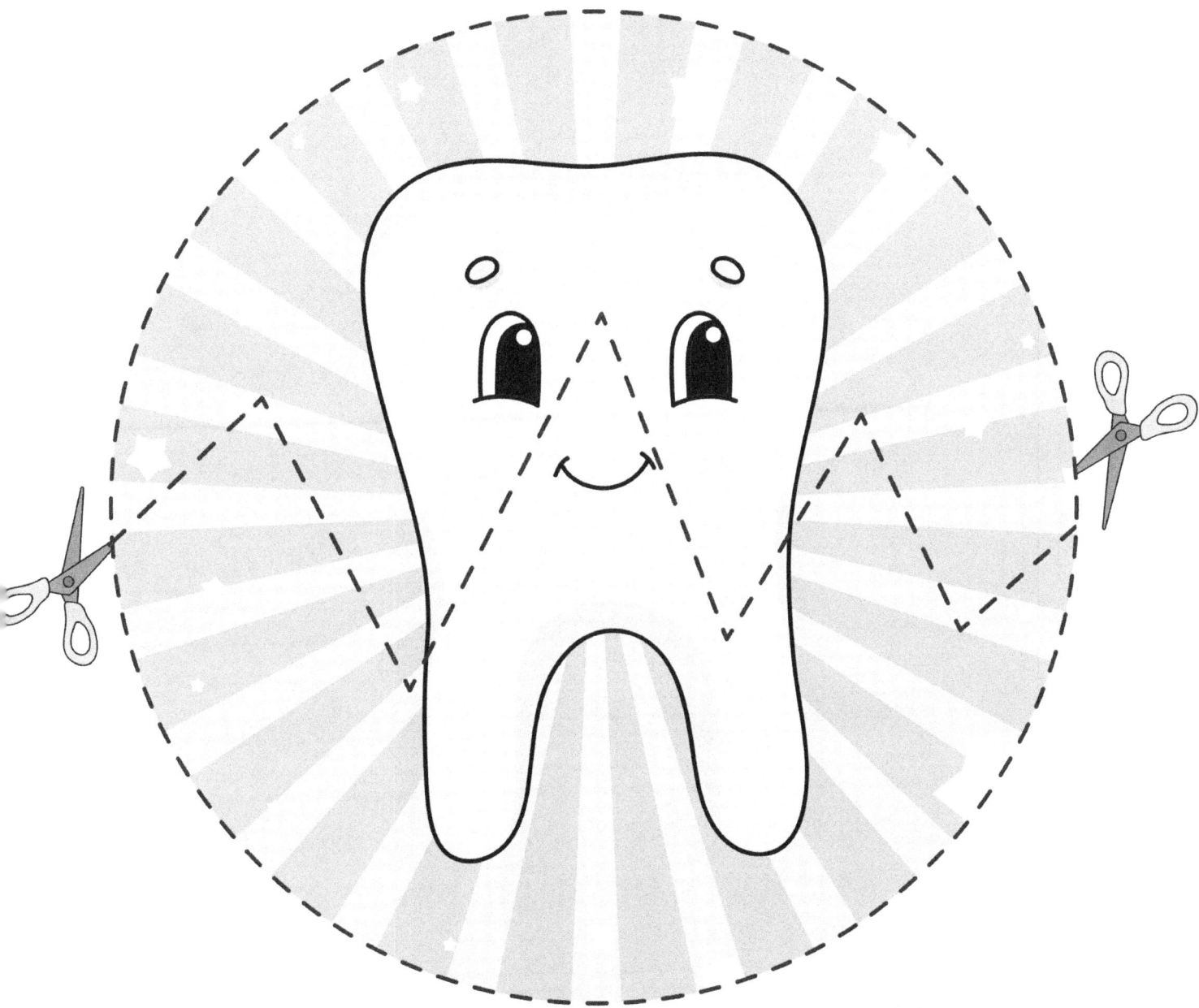

Cut out the picture without running over it with the scissors.

Connect the dots in any way you like and
cut out the drawn shape.

A B C D E F G H I J K L M N O P Q R S T U V W X Y Z ? & !

Cut out the letters and make some interesting words out of them.

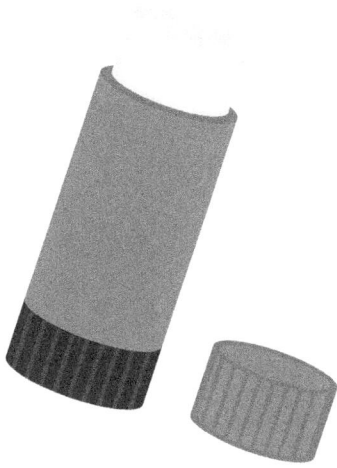

A little reminder of shapes to cut, but now they are smaller because you know how to cut better.

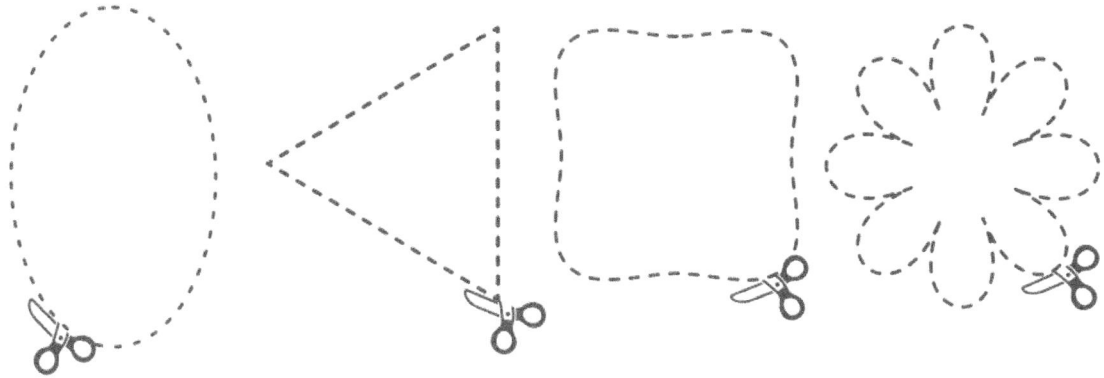

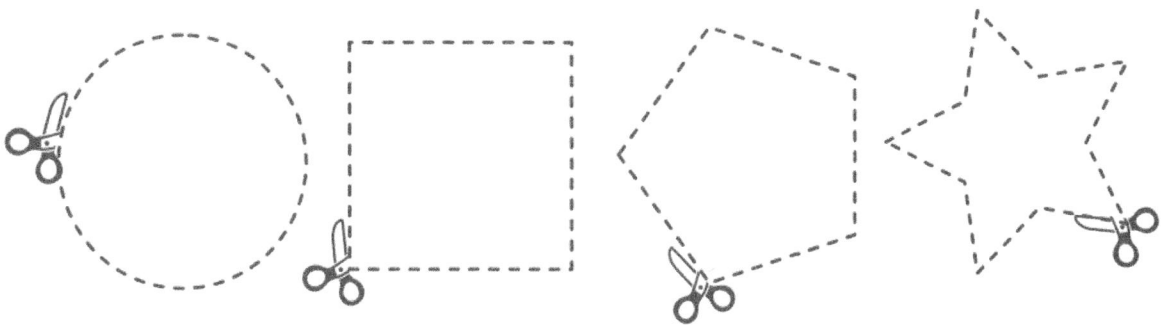

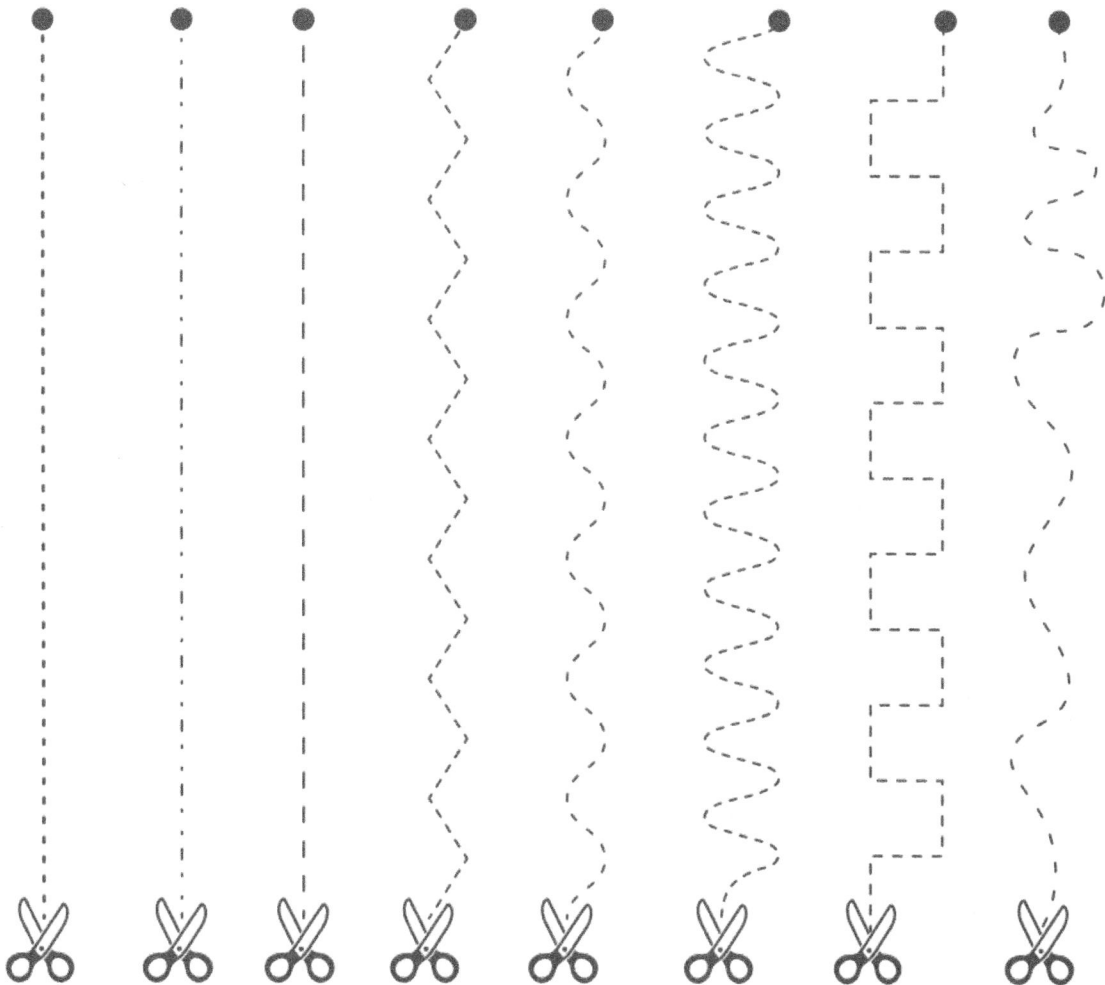

Color and cut each house separately.

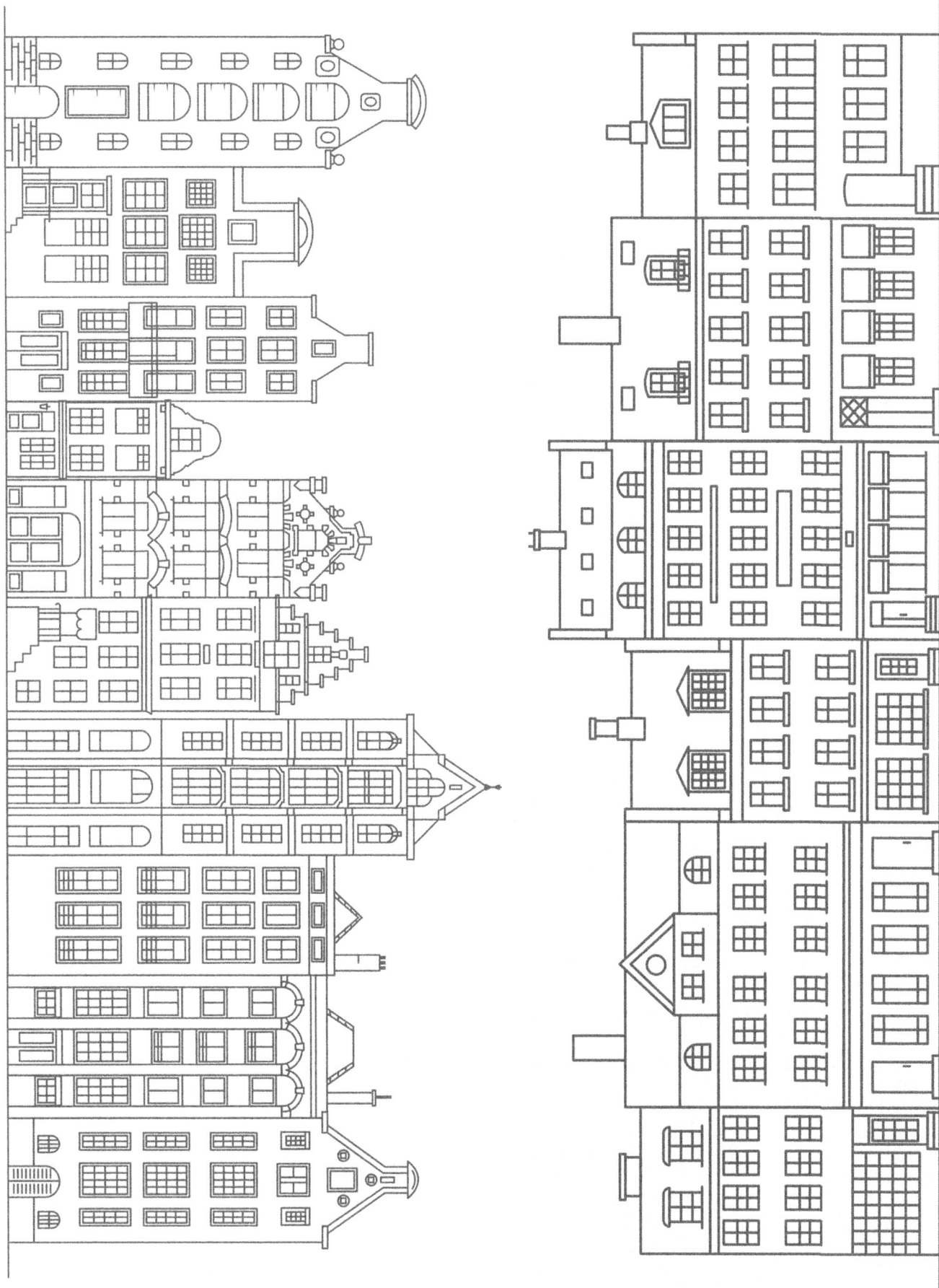

FL

SC

AL

IA

MS

NC

AR

GA

DE

TN

VT OH

CT

MD

OK

PA

NJ

VT

RI

OH

WI

ME

CA

N

MN

MI

MA

L

WV

ND

WY

PA

MO

VA

SD

NE

KS

TX

MT

D

NH

CO

NM

WA

OR

NY

NV

UT

AZ

KY

List the names of the states in their places, then cut along the borders and mix them, then arrange them correctly.

USA

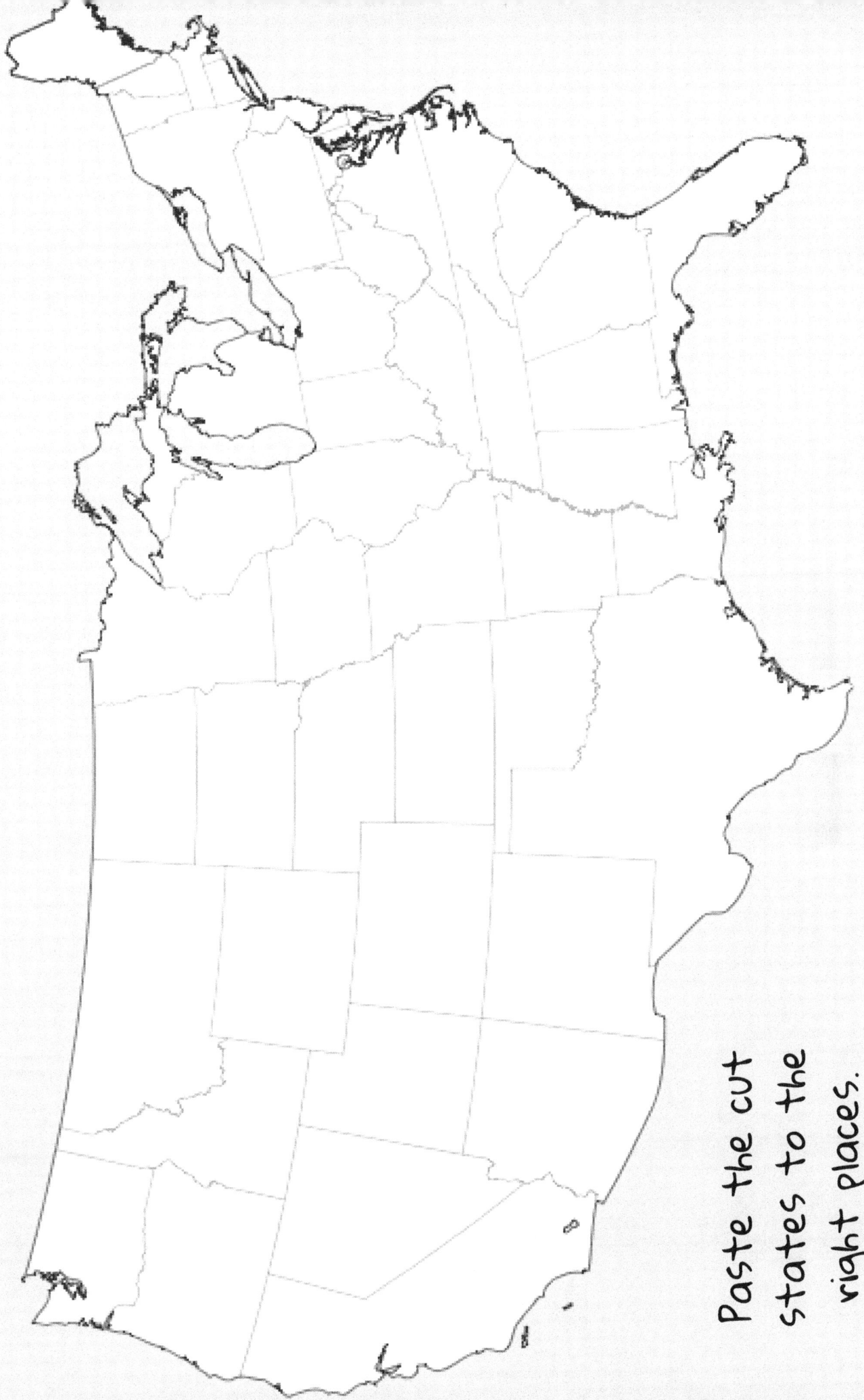

Paste the cut
states to the
right places.

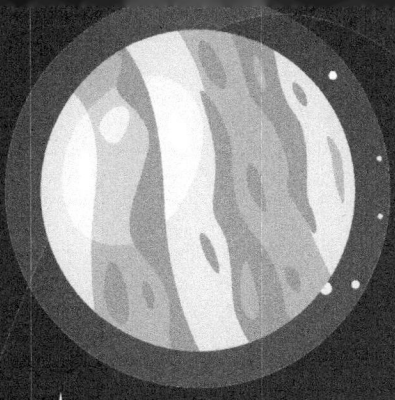 VENUS

 SATURN

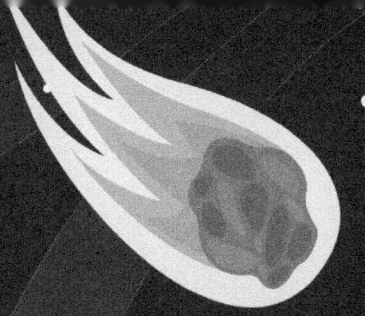 COMET

 JUPITER

 URANUS

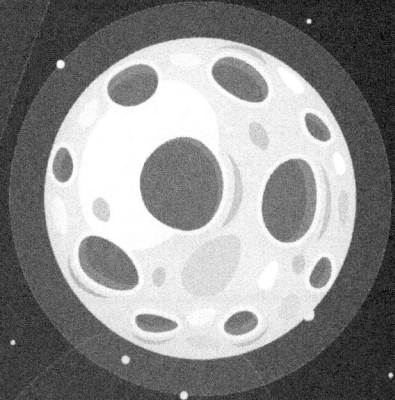 MOON

 EARTH

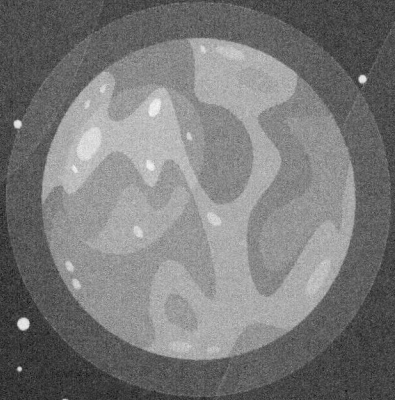 MARS

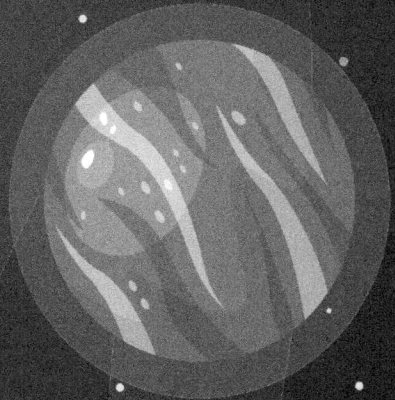 NEPTUN

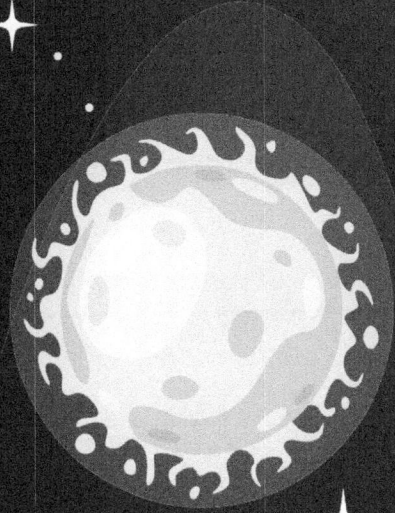 SUN

 MERCURY

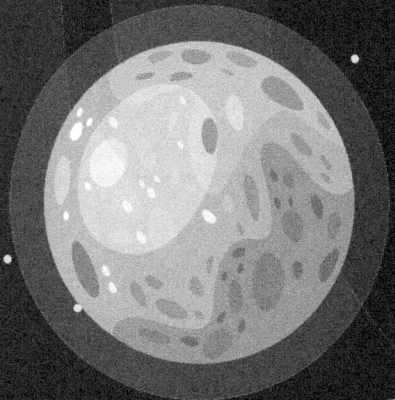 PLUTO

Cut out the planets on the previous page and put them in the correct order here.

Star

Earth satellite

dwarf planet

Cut the garbage and throw it into the appropriate bins.

PAPER   GLASS   METAL   E-WASTE   PLASTIC   ORGANIC

Color and cut.

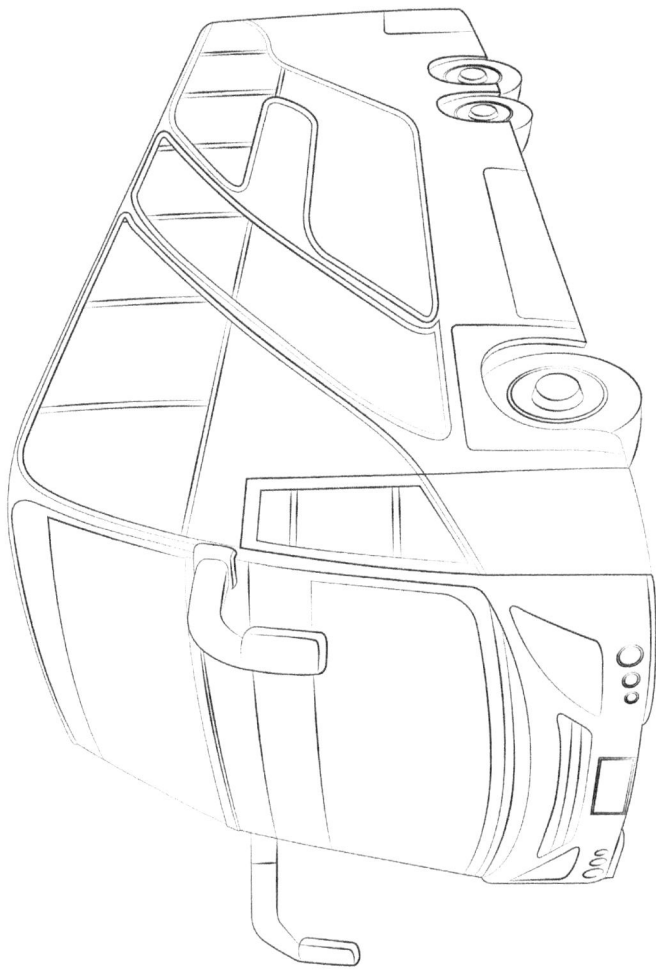

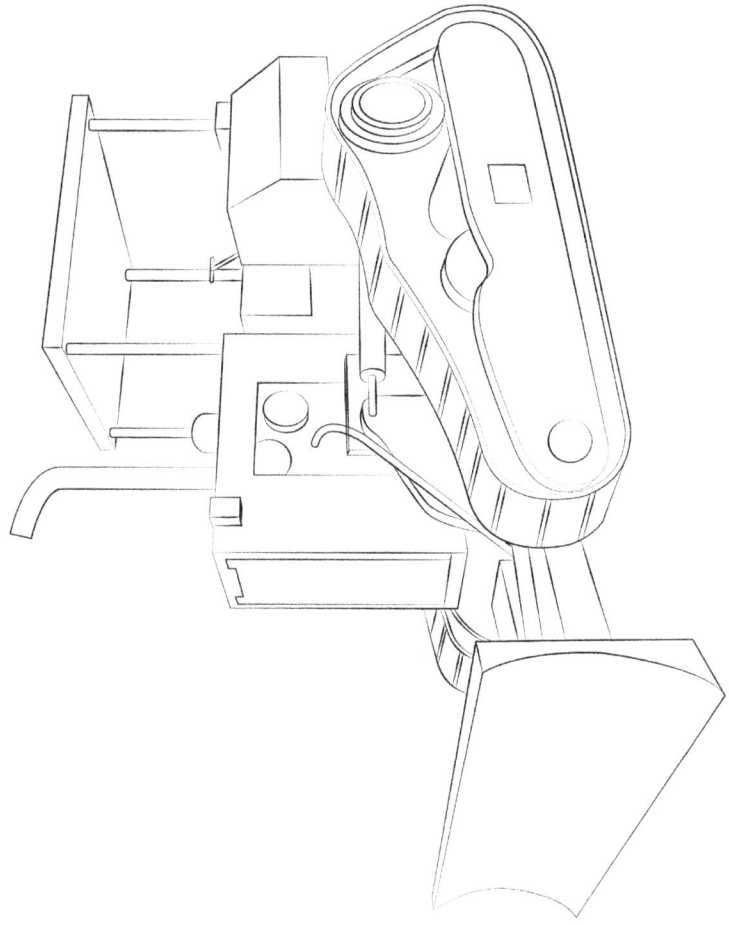

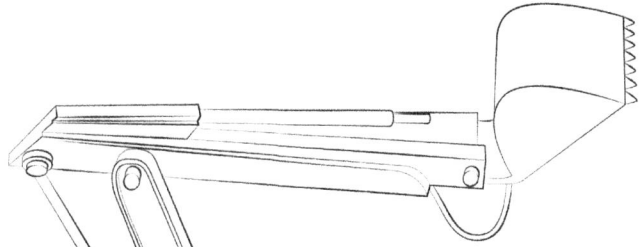

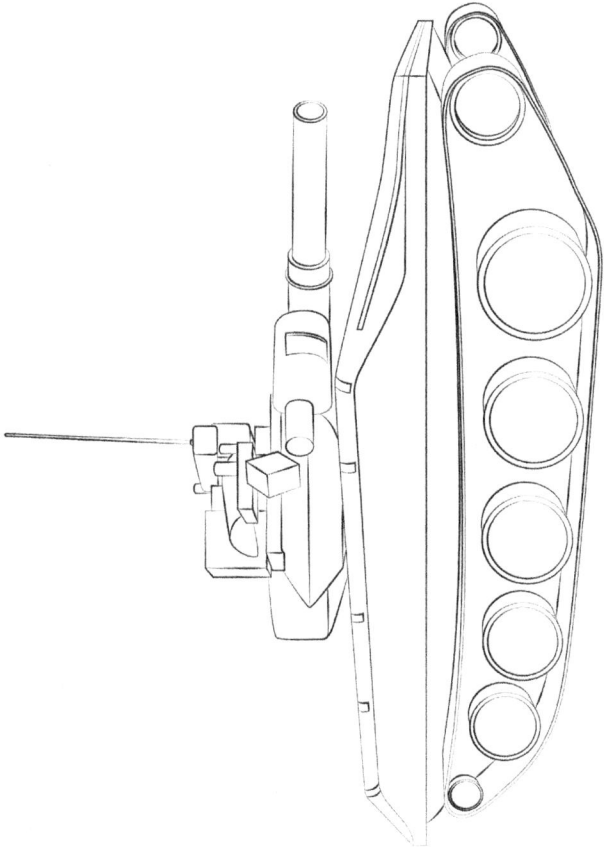

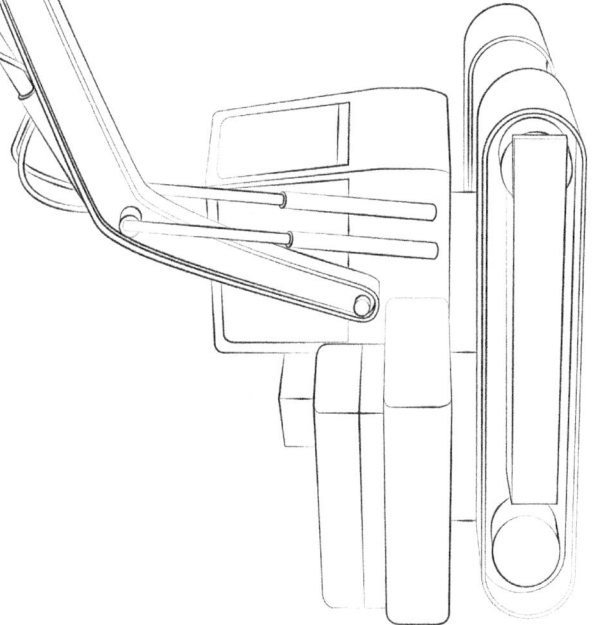

Cut and paste.

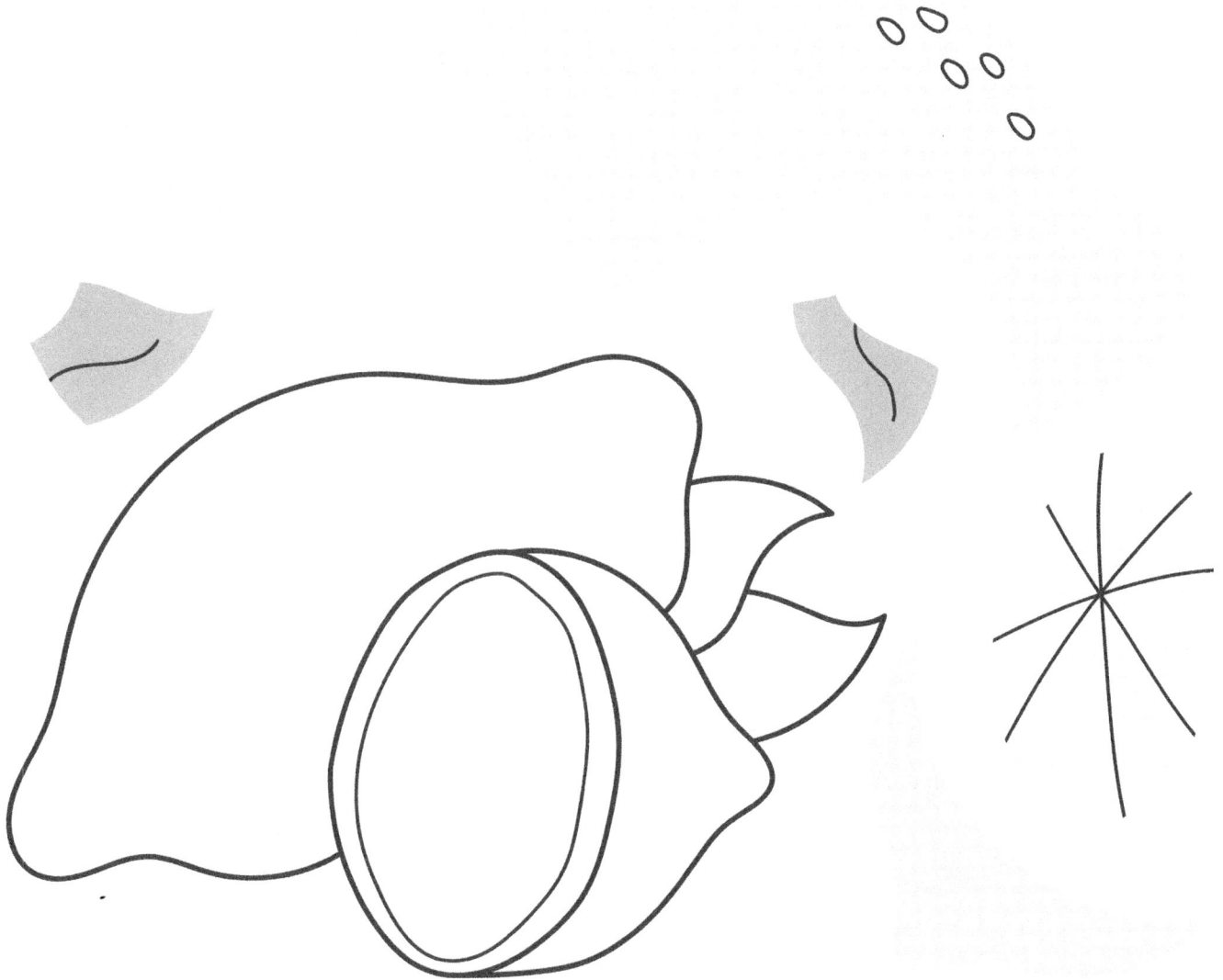

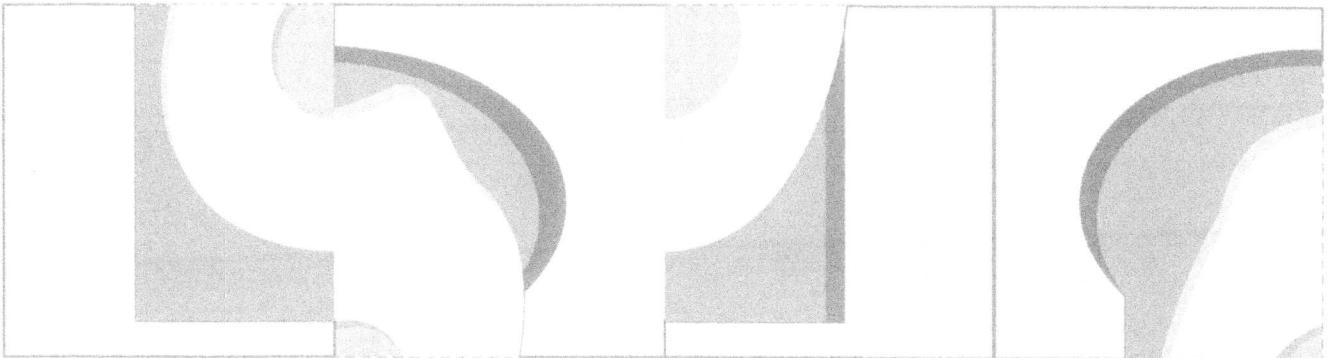

This is the last stage of your learning, now we will see how you did things that you have to cut out here will be smaller than before and will have more difficult shapes.

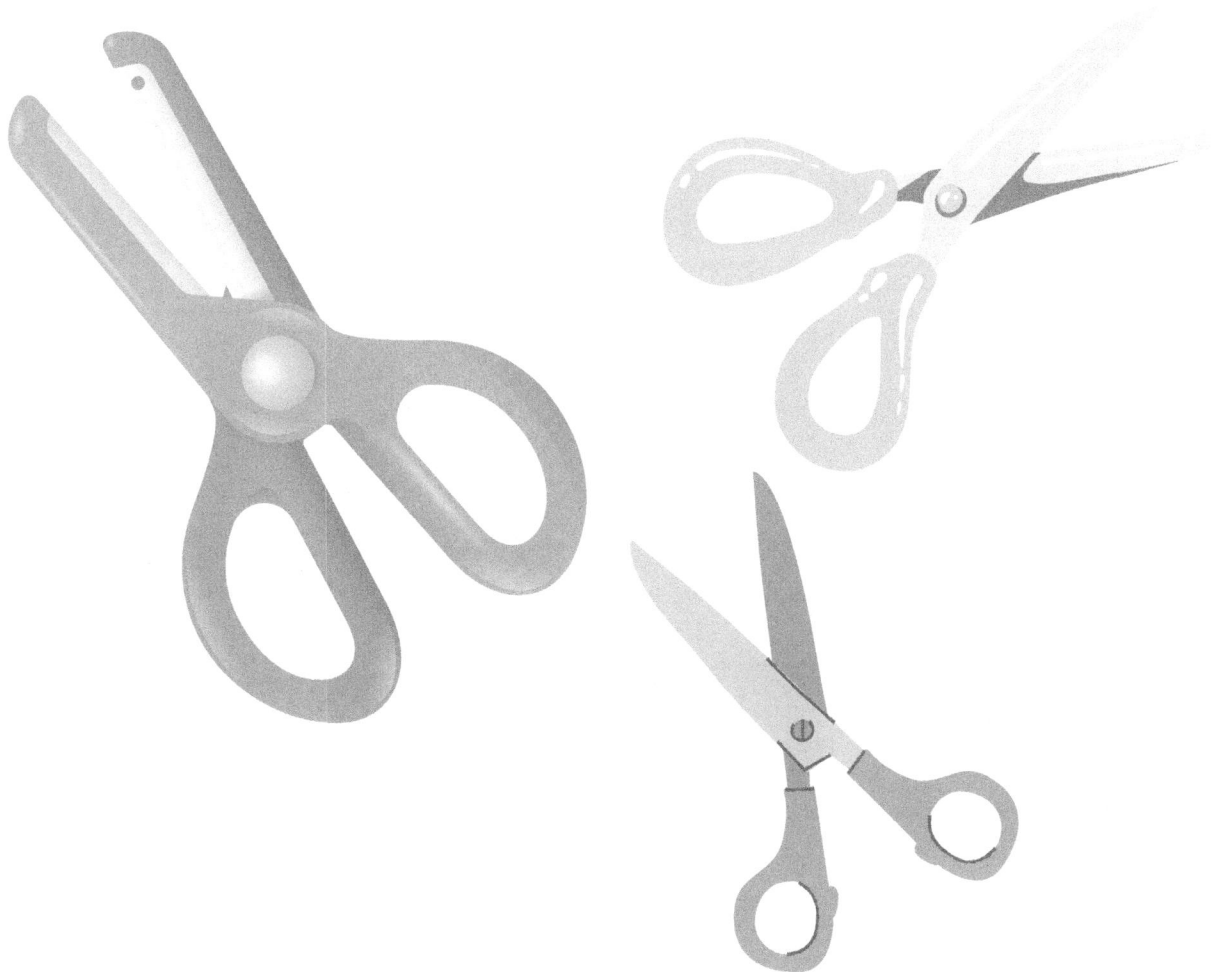

Something easy to start with. Match the pictures according to the numbers.

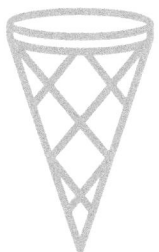

Cut out the animals.

Cut out the animals.

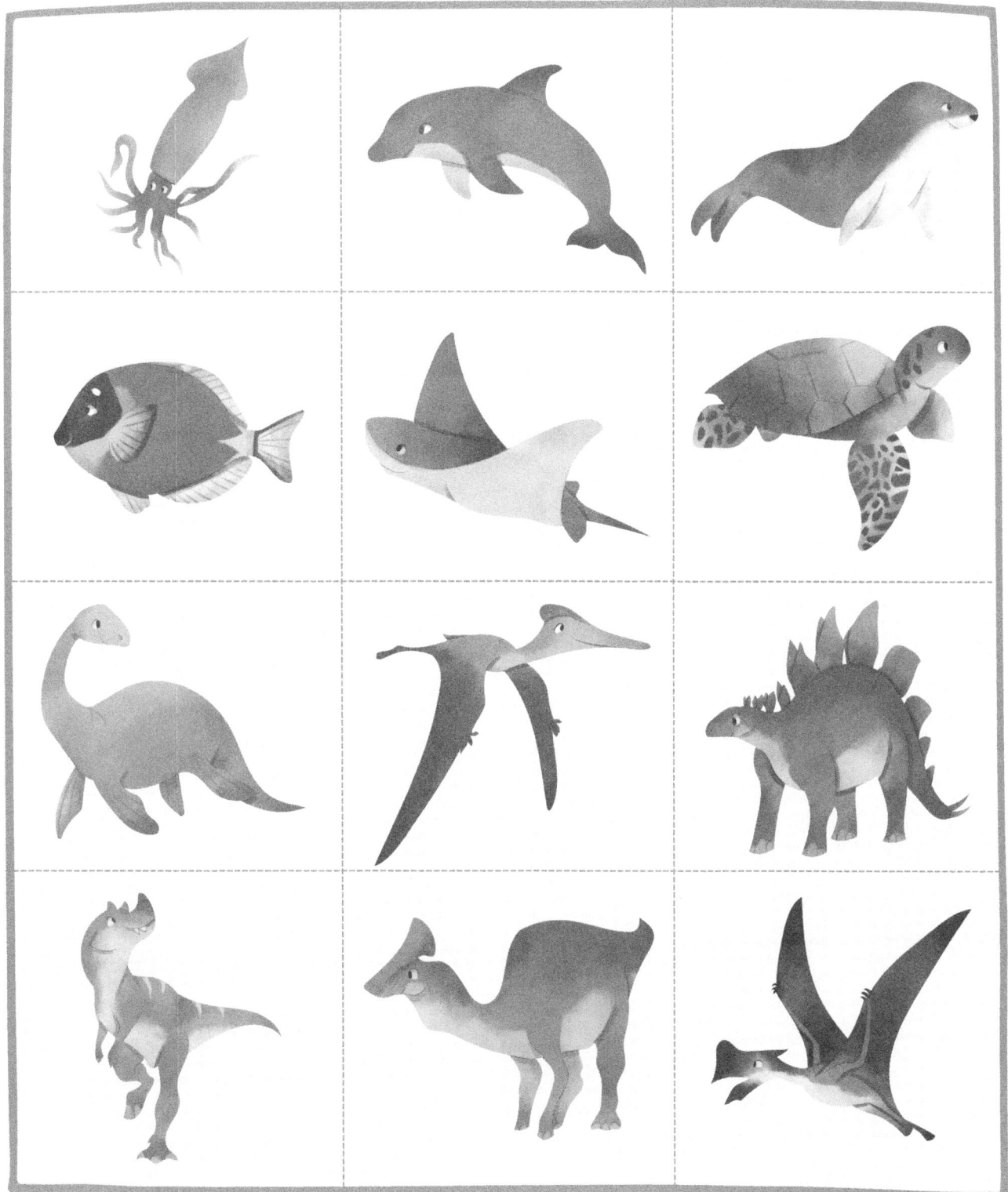

Congratulations

You have gained valuable knowledge, you know how to cut things out of paper.

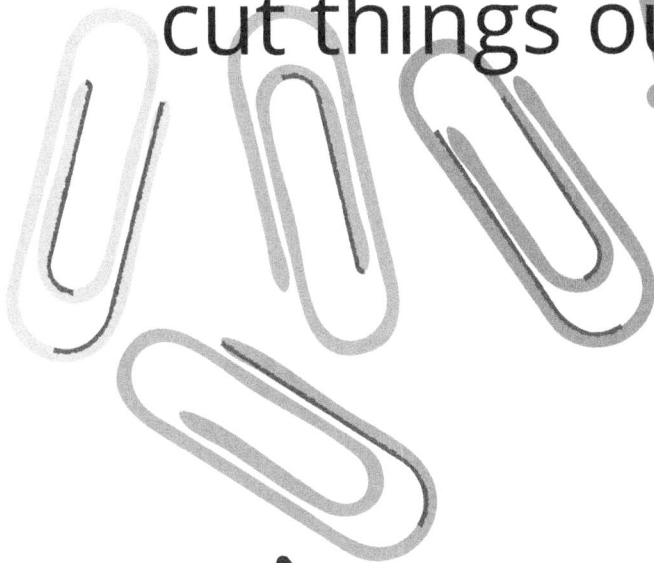

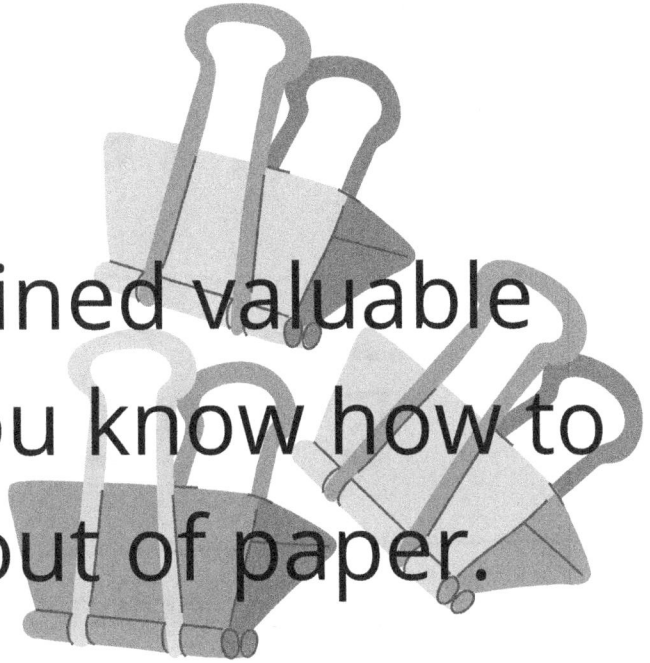

Thank You!

Want Free goodies ?!

E-MAIL US AT:

franciskimmons@gmail.com

or

SCAN QR-CODE

Every opinion is important!

We want to improve, and this requires your opinion, which is worth its weight in gold. If you appreciate our work, please leave feedback for you, it is not much, and for us it is a lever of development.

THANK YOU

THANK YOU

Made in the USA
Las Vegas, NV
18 June 2023